Minnesota
Facts and Symbols

by Bill McAuliffe

Consultant:
William E. Lass
Professor of History
Minnesota State University, Mankato

Hilltop Books
an imprint of Franklin Watts
A Division of Grolier Publishing
New York   London   Hong Kong   Sydney
Danbury, Connecticut

Hilltop Books
http://publishing.grolier.com

Library of Congress Cataloging-in-Publication Data
McAuliffe, Bill.
    Minnesota facts and symbols/Bill McAuliffe.
    p. cm.—(The states and their symbols)
    Includes bibliographical references and index.
    Summary: Presents information about the state of Minnesota, its nickname, motto, and
emblems.
    ISBN 0-7368-0219-3
    1. Emblems, State—Minnesota—Juvenile literature. [1. Emblems, State—Minnesota.
2. Minnesota.] I. Title. II. Series: McAuliffe, Emily. States and their symbols.
CR203.M6M38   1999
977.6—dc21   98-43014
                                                                                         CIP
                                                                                          AC

Editorial Credits
Blanche R. Bolland, editor; Steve Christensen, cover designer; Linda Clavel, illustrator;
    Kimberly Danger and Sheri Gosewisch, photo researchers

Photo Credits
Doris J. Brookes, 22 (middle)
G. Alan Nelson, 18
John Elk III, 10, 22 (bottom)
Karlene V. Schwartz, 14
Kay Shaw Photography, 12
Meggy Becker/David Clobes Stock Photography, 22 (top)
One Mile Up, Inc., 8, 10 (inset)
Robert McCaw, 16
Sage Productions, 20
Unicorn Stock Photos/Ed Harp, 6
Visuals Unlimited/Stephen J. Lang, cover

Table of Contents

Fast Facts

Capital: St. Paul is the capital of Minnesota.

Largest City: Minneapolis is Minnesota's largest city. More than 354,000 people live in Minneapolis.

Size: Minnesota covers 84,068 square miles (217,736 square kilometers). It is the 12th-largest state.

Location: Minnesota lies in the north-central United States. Minnesota shares a border with Canada.

Population: About 4,685,549 people live in Minnesota (U.S. Census Bureau, 1997 estimate).

Statehood: Minnesota became the 32nd state on May 11, 1858.

Natural Resources: Minnesota has wood, iron ore, granite, and limestone.

Manufactured Goods: Minnesota workers make computers, scientific instruments, and machinery.

Crops: Minnesota farmers grow corn, soybeans, sugar beets, and wheat. They also raise dairy cows, hogs, turkeys, and chickens.

State Name and Nickname

The name Minnesota comes from two Native American words. "Minne" means water in the Dakota language. "Sota" means sky-tinted or cloudy. The Dakota used these words to describe the Minnesota River.

The nickname North Star State is closely tied to the state government. The words "north" and "star" are in the state motto. Part of Minnesota reaches farther north than any state except Alaska.

Settlers in the 1800s first called Minnesota the Land of 10,000 Lakes. They hoped this nickname would draw more people to the state.

The nickname Gopher State came from a newspaper cartoon. Four businesses used state money to build railroads in Minnesota in 1858. But they did not finish the railroads. A cartoon compared these businesses to gophers. Gophers sometimes eat farmers' crops. The businesses ate the state's money.

One of Minnesota's nicknames is Land of 10,000 Lakes. But Minnesota actually has 15,291 lakes.

7

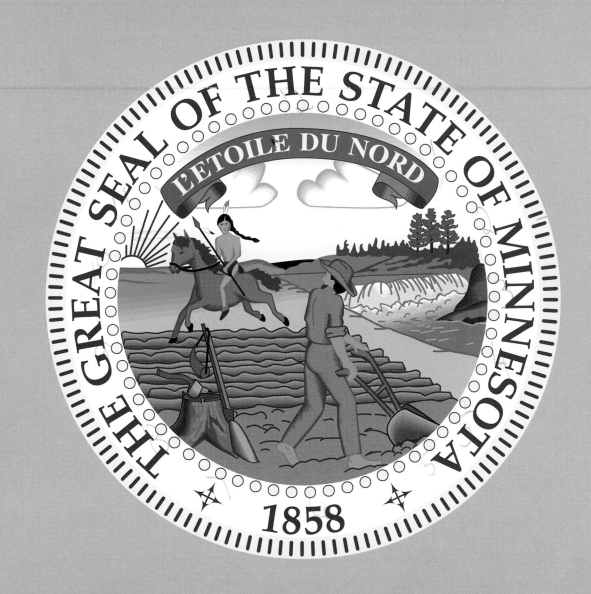

State Seal and Motto

Minnesota adopted its state seal in 1861. The state seal reminds Minnesotans of their state's government. The seal also makes government papers official.

Minnesota's seal shows a Native American on horseback. This figure represents the first people in Minnesota. The seal also shows a farmer plowing a field. The farmer stands for the importance of farming to Minnesota.

A tree stump and a waterfall also appear on the seal. The tree stump stands for lumber. Cutting trees for lumber was one of Minnesota's first businesses. Waterfalls once were important for making flour and lumber. The force of the falling water turned mill wheels to grind wheat or cut boards.

Minnesota's French motto means Star of the North. Minnesota adopted the state motto in 1861.

Pictures on Minnesota's state seal represent the state's history.

State Capitol and Flag

The state capitol building is in St. Paul. St. Paul is Minnesota's capital city. Government officials meet in the capitol to make the state's laws.

Builders finished the state capitol in 1905. The building cost $4.5 million. The capitol's white dome is 223 feet (68 meters) tall.

A golden statue sits on the roof below the dome. Four horses pull a man in a cart. The horses stand for earth, fire, water, and wind. The man in the cart represents growth. Two women lead the horses. The women stand for farming and business.

Minnesota's government approved the state flag in 1957. Minnesota's flag is blue with the state seal in the middle. A ring of lady slippers surrounds the seal. The pink and white lady slipper is Minnesota's state flower. A circle of 19 stars surrounds the flowers. Minnesota was the 19th state after the 13 original states to join the United States.

Minnesota's capitol is in St. Paul.

State Bird

The common loon became Minnesota's state bird in 1961. The loon is the oldest kind of bird still living. Loons lived 60 million years ago. The loon's name comes from a Norwegian word that means wild, sad cry.

Loons make different sounds. They wail to communicate with one another. Members of a pair hoot to show their bond. Loons make a trembling, laughing sound when they sense danger. Males yodel to warn others away. The yodel changes rapidly between high and low sounds.

The common loon is more than 2 feet (61 centimeters) long. Loons can spread their wings up to 5 feet (1.5 meters). They are fast flyers.

Loons also are good divers. They can remain underwater for about five minutes. Loons have red eyes that allow them to see well underwater. They can find food even in deep water.

More than 12,000 loons spend the summer in Minnesota. Loon chicks can swim soon after they hatch.

State Tree

In 1953, officials chose the red pine as Minnesota's state tree. The tree's name comes from the color of its bark.

The red pine is common in states that border the Great Lakes. The tree also grows in the northeastern United States.

Most red pines are about 90 feet (27 meters) tall. The tallest red pine in Minnesota measures 120 feet (37 meters) tall. This red pine is about 300 years old. The tree grows in Itasca State Park.

Pine trees have needles instead of leaves. Red pine needles are about 6 inches (15 centimeters) long. The needles grow in pairs. The needles are soft and snap apart when bent.

Pine trees produce cones that hold seeds. Red pines have smooth cones. The cones measure about 2 inches (5 centimeters) long.

Another name for the red pine is the Norway pine.

State Flower

The pink and white lady slipper became Minnesota's state flower in 1902. Another name for this flower is the showy lady slipper.

The lady slipper is one of the largest wildflowers. Some reach a height of 4 feet (1 meter).

The lady slipper grows in wooded areas of eastern and northern Minnesota. The flower grows in wet, spongy ground. The lady slipper needs a special fungus to grow. This plant helps the lady slipper get food from the soil.

The lady slipper is an orchid. This type of flower has colorful blossoms. The blossoms are shaped like a pouch. Lady slippers bloom in June or July in Minnesota.

The pink and white lady slipper is rare. Laws protect it. People are not allowed to pick Minnesota's state flower.

The blossoms of the pink and white lady slipper are shaped like a pouch.

State Fish

Minnesotans chose the walleye as their state fish in 1965. The walleye is mostly green-gold. The underside of the fish is white.

Walleyes live in freshwater lakes or rivers. Most of Minnesota's lakes have some walleyes. But walleyes prefer the largest lakes. They need a lot of space to swim around.

Walleyes are long and thin. Adults measure 1 to 3 feet (30 to 91 centimeters) long. Most weigh between 1.5 and 2 pounds (0.7 and 0.9 kilograms). The biggest walleye caught in Minnesota weighed 17 pounds, 8 ounces (8 kilograms). Many Minnesotans enjoy fishing for walleyes.

Walleyes swim mostly in cloudy water. Less light comes through cloudy water than clear water. Light hurts walleyes' large eyes.

Walleyes eat what they can find and easily catch. Common foods include small fish, insects, and worms.

Many Minnesotans enjoy fishing for walleyes.

More State Symbols

State Gemstone: The Lake Superior agate has been the state gemstone since 1969. Agates are small stones with streaks. The orange colors in the stones come from iron ore.

State Grain: Wild rice became Minnesota's state grain in 1977. Wild rice grows in shallow lakes and marshes in northern Minnesota. All the wild rice produced in the world once came from Minnesota.

State Muffin: Government officials named the blueberry muffin Minnesota's official state muffin in 1988. Blueberries grow wild in wet, spongy ground in northeastern Minnesota.

State Mushroom: The morel became the state mushroom in 1984. Morels often grow near trees.

State Song: "Hail! Minnesota" was the University of Minnesota's school song. Students Truman Rickard and Arthur Upson wrote the song in 1905. "Hail! Minnesota" became the state song in 1945.

Harvesting wild rice is a tradition for many Native Americans in Minnesota.

Places to Visit

Historic Fort Snelling

Fort Snelling shows what frontier life was like around 1826. Guides lead tours and show crafts. They dress in clothes from the 1800s and act out scenes from the past. Visitors join in some activities. A new feature is the 1820s School Day. Children can experience what school was like long ago.

Itasca State Park

The Mississippi River begins as a narrow stream in Itasca State Park. The Mississippi flows out of Lake Itasca. Visitors walk across the mighty Mississippi on small rocks. Some of Minnesota's oldest pine trees grow in Itasca State Park. These red pines grew after a forest fire in 1714.

Minnesota Zoo

The Minnesota Zoo in Apple Valley has about 1,200 animals. These animals live much like they would in the wild. A train on a high railway carries visitors around the zoo. Visitors to Zoolab play with some of the animals. They can pet a snake or talk to an Amazon parrot.

Words to Know

fungus (FUHN-guhss)—a type of plant that has no leaves, flowers, or roots; mushrooms and molds are fungi.

mill wheel (MIL WEEL)—a waterwheel that drives a mill; mills grind wheat into flour and cut boards.

muffin (MUHF-uhn)—a sweet bread shaped like a cupcake

orchid (OR-kid)—a plant with colorful and often unusually shaped flowers

statue (STACH-oo)—a model of a person or an animal made from metal, stone, or wood

yodel (YOH-duhl)—to sing in a voice that changes rapidly between high and low sounds; male loons yodel to defend their territories.

Read More

Fradin, Dennis Brindell, and Judith Bloom Fradin. *Minnesota.* From Sea to Shining Sea. Chicago: Children's Press, 1995.

Joseph, Paul. *Minnesota.* United States. Minneapolis: Abdo & Daughters, 1998.

O'Hara, Megan. *Frontier Fort: Fort Life on the Upper Mississippi, 1826.* Living History. Mankato, Minn.: Blue Earth Books, 1998.

Useful Addresses

Minnesota History Center
345 W. Kellogg Blvd.
St. Paul, MN 55102

Minnesota Office of Tourism
100 Metro Square
121 7th Place East
St. Paul, MN 55101

Internet Sites

Minnesota
http://www.50states.com/minnesot.htm
North Star—Minnesota State Government Online
http://www.state.mn.us
State Symbols
http://www.governor.state.mn.us/new/kidspage/
    statesym.htm

Index

J   McAuliffe, Bill
917.   Minnesota facts and
76   Symbols   and
MCA

$14.00

DATE			